M is for Meow

A Cat Alphabet

Written by Helen L. Wilbur and Illustrated by Robert Papp

Sleeping Bear Press wishes to thank and acknowledge John M. Kruger, DVM, Veterinary Teaching Hospital, Michigan State University, for reading and reviewing the manuscript.

We also extend a special thanks and acknowledgment to our cat models: Ramona Bacheller, Francesca Cruden, Taffy and Fraidy Papp, and Bunster and Nugent Wilbur.

Sleeping Bear Press™
310 North Main Street, Suite 300
Chelsea, MI 48118
www.sleepingbearpress.com

Printed and bound in China.

First Edition

10 9 8 7 6 5 4 3 2 1

Library of Congress Cataloging-in-Publication Data

Wilbur, Helen L., 1948-
M is for meow : a cat alphabet / written by Helen L. Wilbur ; illustrated by Robert Papp.
p. cm.
Summary: "Using the alphabet format, the history, care, behavior, and mystery of cats is presented. Feline facts are also included"—Provided by publisher.
ISBN-13: 978-1-58536-304-9
ISBN-10: 1-58536-304-9
1. Cats. 2. English language—Alphabet. I. Title.

SF442.W82 2007
636.8—dc22 2006023430

For my mother and father, for Myrla, Chris, and Ernie,
and forever for the Bunster.

HELEN

For Lisa, Elsie, and Steve—my favorite fellow cat lovers.

ROBERT

a A

Scientists working with DNA have recently gained more insight into how cats developed from their prehistoric ancestors and migrated around the globe. Early fossil records for cats are few, making tracing the family tree for modern cats difficult. Both cats and dogs are thought to have descended from an ancient precursor *Miacis*, a weasel-like carnivore that lived 45 to 50 million years ago.

The earliest known cat, *Proailurus*, was not much bigger than a modern day house cat. Proailurus lived in Europe 20-30 million years ago. This tree-dwelling predator weighed about 20 pounds, had large eyes, sharp teeth and claws, and a long tail.

Larger cats appeared as mammals began to dominate the earth. These cats, distant cousins of our cats, flourished in the Ice Age throughout most of the world. They ambushed grazing mammals, Mastodons, and Mammoths for food. *Smilodon* ("knife tooth"), called the saber-toothed cat because of its seven-inch fangs, is the best known of these. Scientists know a lot about Smilodon because of the thousands of fossils left in the La Brea Tar Pits in California. These cats became extinct at the end of the Ice Age about 11,000 years ago.

A is for Ancestors and Anatomy

All the cats that came before us,
Saber-toothed and Proailurus,
for millions of years they've proven the fact—
Throughout all time a cat's a cat.

Recent research shows that cats as we know them today evolved rapidly in the last 11 million years. Feline ancestors migrated from Asia to Africa and across the Bering Strait into the Americas, everywhere except Australia and Antarctica, six to eight million years ago.

Modern domestic cats are very similar to their wild ancestors in behavior and anatomy. From earliest times cats were designed for hunting with strong, flexible bodies, sharp claws and teeth, exceptional balance and speed, with the main differences being size. Most all cats also show considerable resemblance in social behavior as solitary hunters coming together only to mate.

While we don't really know the coloration of these early cats, it's likely that environment determined body markings to blend in with surroundings and hide from prey. Cats in grasslands are pale and striped, forest and jungle cats are spotted and darker.

All pet cats belong to the same species, *Felis catus*. Cats come in a wide variety of coat color forms and patterns. Less than three percent of pet cats belong to a specific breed. A breed is a group of cats with common physical features (i.e., body type, eye shape, and face formation) which distinguish it from other breeds. Some breeds have unusual characteristics, like the tailless Manx or the hairless Sphynx.

There are nearly 100 distinct cat breeds recognized by various cat registries worldwide. Breeds are divided into long-haired and short-haired. The Persian cats with their thick coats, fluffy tails, and flat faces make up more than half of registered cats. Some other long-haired breeds are the Maine Coon, Turkish Angora, Himalayan, and Ragdoll. Some short-haired breeds include the Abyssinian, Burmese, Scottish Fold, and Singapura.

In a cat show cats are judged against the ideal characteristics of their breed as set down in the breed standard. Many cat shows have categories for children and for family pets. Without a breed standard, judges look for healthy, handsome household cats.

B b

B is for Breed

Long-haired, short-haired, calico, Angora,
Burmese, Siamese, Maine Coon, Singapura,
a little lost kitten or a splendid pedigreed—
Every kind of feline makes a fine pet indeed.

Cc

In recent years cats have surpassed dogs as the most popular household pet. Despite their independent ways, cats make devoted, affectionate companions.

Cats make good pets for the elderly and people who live alone because they are less active and require less care than other household pets. Stroking a cat is known to reduce blood pressure and relieve stress. Some cats live in nursing homes and hospitals as therapy animals where their friendship alleviates loneliness and assists in healing.

Cats have also been companions to lives of adventure. Trim was born in 1797 on the HMS *Reliance* on its way to Australia. Matthew Flinders, the ship's captain, saw the kitten fall overboard, swim back to the ship, and climb aboard on a rope. Trim became the favorite of Captain Flinders and the crew, sailing with them around Australia and surviving a shipwreck. Celebrated by Captain Flinders as the "most affectionate of friends, faithful of servants, and best of creatures," Trim's statue sits on the window ledge of the Mitchell Library in Sydney, Australia.

C is for Companion

Soft as butter, sweet as cream,
dear Companion sleep and dream
upon my lap like a caress,
filled with warmth and tenderness.

Cats have lived with humans for a much shorter time than other domestic animals. When people started growing and storing grain, they welcomed cats into their settlements to control the mice and rats. The first record of non-native cats in human settlements is in Cyprus 8,000 years ago.

Exactly when cats became tame household animals is not known. Egyptian tomb paintings show cats as an integral part of daily life, and ancient Egyptians regarded cats as sacred animals.

Where people went, cats went. The Roman army took cats with them on campaigns to protect their provisions. Popular for pest control on early sailing ships, cats spread throughout the world. Cats came to the Americas with Columbus and we know that at least one cat was on the *Mayflower*.

Dd

D is for Domestication

Welcomed into home and farm
by the fire so snug and warm.
Every comfort has its price.
Cats are here to catch the mice.

Ee

People are rarely indifferent to cats. They either adore them or dislike them. Cat lovers are called *ailurophiles* (from the Greek *ailouros* which means "cat" and *phile*, "love").

Cats live life on their own terms. Closer than other domestic animals to their lives as wild creatures, cats remain elusive and self-possessed. Even the tamest household cat retains the mystery and spirit of the tiger in the jungle. Cat lovers delight in sharing their lives with these beautiful, serene, and often contradictory creatures which make loyal, loving, and playful companions.

Famous cat lovers come from all eras and walks of life. Winston Churchill, prime minister of Britain, loved his cats. Jock, his favorite marmalade cat, ate meals with Sir Winston and was with him when he died. In his will Churchill specified that there should always be a marmalade cat named Jock at his home, Chartwell, in Kent, England, and there is. Other noted ailurophiles include Robert E. Lee, Abraham Lincoln, Leonardo da Vinci, Albert Einstein, Florence Nightingale, and Andy Warhol.

E is for Enthusiast

Mysterious and solitary;
elegant, somewhat contrary.
Asleep upon the pillow purring.
Why do we find you so alluring?

Who is the most famous cat in America? Some might say Morris, the orange 'spokes-cat' for Purina 9 Lives cat food. Since 1968 three cats have played the finicky Morris. The original Morris rose to fame from life in a Chicago cat shelter. Morris has appeared in movies, written books, and even ran for president!

Cats in literature have charmed readers since *Puss in Boots* was written in the 1600s. They might be clever and adventurous like Dr. Seuss's *The Cat in the Hat* or badly behaved like Jack Ganto's *Rotten Ralph*. What would Alice's Wonderland have been without the Cheshire Cat?

Krazy Kat appeared as the first cartoon cat in 1910 in *The Dingbats*, later getting his own cartoon strip with Ignatz Mouse. Felix the cat was the first cat movie star in *Adventures of Felix* in 1919 and was the first cat on television. NBC used a papier-mâché statue of Felix as the black-and-white test pattern for broadcasts in 1928.

From Garfield to Sylvester to Catbert, cat characters have charmed, infuriated, and entertained us.

Ff

F is for Famous Felines

No paparazzi, no large staffs,
no doing lunch, no autographs.
But on the screen and on TVs
cats are fabulous celebrities.

Gg

G is for Grooming

Keeping fur smooth, clean, and sleek.
Maintaining whiskers at their peak.
Grooming eliminates all flaws
for shining tails and tidy paws.

A kitten's first experience is being licked and cleaned by its mother. Mother cats groom their kittens for cleanliness and bonding. A kitten starts to groom itself when it is about three weeks old.

Cats groom themselves using a specific sequence. They lick their paws to moisten them and rub the wet paw over the head and ears. They then groom their legs and bodies, finishing at the tip of the tail. The rough surface of a cat's tongue is perfect for cleaning fur. Cats munch at matted hair and between their paws to remove dirt. Cats living together groom one another for social interaction as well as hygiene in hard-to-reach areas behind the ears.

As well as keeping a cat clean, grooming gives fur insulating and waterproofing qualities, eliminates shed fur, and acts as a cooling agent in the heat. Hairballs occur when cats throw up fur collected in the stomach. Brushing helps eliminate hairballs, especially in the spring when cats shed their winter coats. Most house cats enjoy being brushed by their human companions and may lick them to return the favor.

H is for Hunter

Still and silent, crouched to the ground,
listening for the smallest sound.
Waiting and watching in the dark house,
the cat sees you, unlucky mouse!

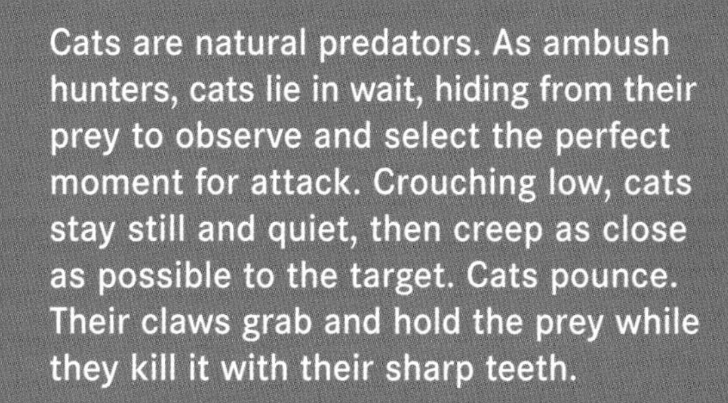

Cats are natural predators. As ambush hunters, cats lie in wait, hiding from their prey to observe and select the perfect moment for attack. Crouching low, cats stay still and quiet, then creep as close as possible to the target. Cats pounce. Their claws grab and hold the prey while they kill it with their sharp teeth.

Smell, sight, and hearing help cats determine the location of their quarry. Their large eyes give them a wide field of vision with an excellent ability to detect motion. Cats do not really "see in the dark," but they do see very well in dim light.

Cats have exceptional hearing, especially for high-pitched sounds like those a bird or mouse makes. Their large external ears rotate to locate and identify sounds. They hear sounds at greater distances than humans, which is why they seem to know when someone is coming long before you do.

When feeding your cat, remember that cats are carnivores. Cats require meat. A vegetarian diet will not provide a cat with sufficient nutrition to remain healthy.

Ii

Why is there a connection between cats and books? Reading and writing are solitary and contemplative acts perfectly suited for the quiet and soothing personality associated with a cat.

The lonely pursuit of writing makes cats ideal companions for authors. Many famous writers celebrated their cat companions, among them Charles Dickens, T. S. Eliot, Edgar Allen Poe, Raymond Chandler, Mark Twain, Vladimir Nabokov, and Ernest Hemingway.

Originally (and mistakenly) named William, Charles Dickens's (1812-1870) cat, Willamena, gave birth to kittens in his study. Dickens was determined not to keep them but one little white kitten won his heart. Known as Master's Cat, she stayed with him when he wrote, snuffing out his reading candle when she wanted attention.

Ernest Hemingway (1899-1961) lived an active and robust life as a sportsman as well as a writer. A ship's captain gave Hemingway a six-toed (polydactyl) cat. Hemingway liked the company of cats and had many of them at his homes in Key West, Florida and Havana, Cuba. Today you can see some of the descendants of Hemingway's original cats among the 60 or so cats that live at the Hemingway Home and Museum in Key West.

I is for Inspiration

Cats have been an inspiration
for those who write as a vocation.
They're also found in cozy nooks
in libraries and stores for books.

Cats have been a favorite subject of artists of all eras from the regal Egyptian cat statues to the posters of Theophile Steinlen. Many famous artists portrayed the beauty and personality of cats, including Leonardo da Vinci, Paul Gauguin, Édouard Manet, Pablo Picasso, and Pierre-Auguste Renoir.

Composers, too, have taken inspiration from their feline friends. Domenico Scarlatti based the musical theme for "The Cat's Fugue" on his cat Pulcinella's prancing on the keys of his harpsichord. Ballet, modern, and jazz dancers study and imitate the graceful movements of cats. The great choreographer George Balanchine was an ardent cat lover.

Many bookstores and libraries make homes for cats to control the rodent population and assist readers. Probably the two most recognized library cats are the marble lions guarding the entrance to the New York Public Library on Fifth Avenue. In the 1930s New York City Mayor Fiorello La Guardia named the lions Patience and Fortitude.

All cats belong to the family *Felidae*. There are about 40 species of wild cats, from the 500-pound Asian tiger to the four-pound rusty spotted cat. Big cats (*Pantherinae*) include lions, tigers, jaguars, leopards, and snow leopards. Cheetahs are big cats which belong to a separate group called *Acinonychinae*. There are many varieties of smaller or lesser cats (*Felinae*) throughout the world, such as the ocelot, margay, lynx, caracal, serval, jaguarundi, and bobcat.

What separates a small from a big cat? Zoologists don't group them by size alone. Big cats tend to have round pupils, eat lying down, and have a throat structure which allows them to roar. Lion roars can be heard as far as five miles away!

Cats in the wild are solitary, nocturnal hunters with the exception of lions which live and hunt in a group called a pride.

Most wild cat species are threatened by habitat loss and human hunting. Zoos provide protection, safety, and study, along with breeding programs often matching mates from long distances, ensuring that the species continue with healthy cats.

Jj

J is for Jaguar

Majestic beasts, untamed and proud;
ferocious and beautiful with grace endowed.
Relentlessly stalking the plains afar—
The lion, the cheetah, the jaguar.

K is for Kitten

Chase your tail, leap so high,
roll about, stalk a fly.
Take a nap, wake up, eat.
Get a snuggle, then repeat.

Born blind and deaf with eyes shut and ears flattened to their heads, newborn kittens weigh about three to five ounces. They depend completely on their mother. Their eyes don't open for seven to ten days and their ears unfold in two weeks, yet newborns' strong sense of smell guides them to their mother's milk. One of a cat's earliest reflexes is the kneading motion of a kitten's paws to stimulate milk flow.

As kittens grow and their senses develop, they begin to play and explore the world. Play socializes kittens and mimics the skills they will need to become self-sufficient hunters. Pouncing, chasing, and jumping develop the coordination, strength, and agility kittens will need to catch prey and defend themselves.

Kittens are ready to leave their mothers when they are about 12 weeks old. When selecting one as a pet, make sure that it is healthy and lively, with a clean, dry coat, a firm body, clear ears, and clean eyes, nose, and mouth. An outgoing kitten used to being handled by people is a good bet for a future pet.

Throughout the ages cats have been both worshipped and vilified.

Ancient Egyptians regarded cats as sacred animals. Bastet, the household goddess of family, fertility, and pleasure, protected women, children, and domestic cats. Statues and paintings show her with the head of a cat and the body of a woman. The Egyptian word for cat was "miu" or "mau." Cats were so highly regarded in Egypt that they were mummified and buried in cat cemeteries with embalmed mice. The penalty for killing a cat was death.

Viking legend portrays Freya, the goddess of love, fertility, and war, in a chariot drawn by two huge cats. Viking brides often received kittens as essential gifts for their new households.

In Islamic tradition the cat was born in Noah's ark from the lion's sneeze. The prophet Mohammed (570-632) was fond of cats. Once when called to prayer, Mohammed found his pet cat Muezza sound asleep on the sleeve of his robe. Rather than disturb the cat, he cut off the sleeve.

Ll

L is for Legends and Lore

In ancient Egypt the feline
was treated as a god divine.
That's why a cat which sits and thinks
reminds us of the Nile's Sphinx.

In the Middle Ages in Europe cats became associated with witchcraft and sorcery. Witches supposedly took the form of black cats at night. Cats were often persecuted as agents of the devil and omens of bad luck.

Superstitions about cats survive to this day. Cats are said to be forecasters of visitors, luck, weather, crops, death, and the likelihood or success of marriages, among other things. In different cultures black cats symbolize both good and bad luck. A cat's sneeze might bring such varying things as rain, company, good luck, or a happy marriage.

Cat sayings

- *To let the cat out of the bag* is to tell a secret.
- *It's like herding cats* means that it's a task of organization that's impossible to accomplish.
- *Another breed of cats* means it's something entirely different.
- The *cat's meow, cat's whiskers*, or *cat's pajamas* are things that are unusual or exceptional.

Cat proverbs

- Curiosity killed the cat.
- When the cat is away the mice will play.
- When rats infest the palace, a lame cat is better than the swiftest horse.
- One should not send a cat to deliver cream.

M m

Cats communicate with one another using body language, scent, and sound. They mew at their mothers as kittens but as adults use the sound we know as "meow" for communicating with their human companions. Cats meow to get what they want from us. The pitch, tone, and length of a meow signal its meaning from a calm "hello" to an urgent "help me."

Cats make other sounds besides meow. A mother cat uses a special chirping sound to call her kittens. House cats often greet their owners with this friendly sound. When observing prey, a cat will frequently crouch and make a chattering noise. Angry cats, ready to fight or defend themselves, growl, hiss, snarl, and spit. Cats in pain make a low-pitched yowl or caterwaul when calling for a mate.

People who live with cats learn to understand what a particular meow means. A high-pitched pleasant meow may be a simple plea for attention and play, while a demanding meow by the door can mean "let me out, now!"

Do you know what your cat is telling you?

M is for Meow

Feed me, pet me, come and play.
Let me out, please go away!
A cat fits all these thoughts somehow
into the tiny word *MEOW*.

cat lives in an entirely different world
f smells than we do. With a sense of
mell 14 times stronger than a human's,
cat uses smell as the primary way to
xplore and identify its environment. Smell
elps a cat find food, locate a mate, mark
erritory, and detect danger.

cat's nose has millions more scent-
nalyzing cells than ours. Plus, a cat has
special organ for sensing smells in the
oof of its mouth called a vomero-nasal or
acobson's organ. When a cat stops, opens
s mouth into something like a smile,
nd inhales with its eyes half closed, it
getting intense odor information about
s world.

mell, more than taste, determines a
at's reaction to its food. Cats have a weak
ense of taste with only 473 taste buds,
ompared to 9,000 for a human. A sick
at, particularly one with the cat equiva-
ent of a head cold, may not be able to
mell its food. It will find it more tempting
you warm it up.

N n

N is for Nose

Whiskers twitching, ears erect,
sniffing things we can't detect.
You'd be amazed what a cat can tell
inhaling deep with one good smell.

O is for Out

Cats go out and then want in—
Once in, they must go out again.
One thing that we know for sure;
cats just do not like a door.

Every cat lover has had the experience of closing a door only to have a cat scratch, pace, or howl until it is opened. What may appear as willful behavior actually relates to a cat's need to inspect and patrol its territory.

Cats in the wild are solitary hunters with territories up to 175 acres, depending on the availability of food. Cats mark their territories with scent glands located in the faces, chins, feet, and tails. They regularly check out the network of paths that make up their territory to refresh their landmark and sniff for signs left by other cats. Since domestic cats get fed at home, territory size is less important, especially for indoor cats. But their need to establish and mark territories still remains, particularly in homes with more than one cat.

When a cat rubs against the furniture or your leg in a friendly greeting, it is really leaving scent marking its territory. That's why cats are quick to investigate any changes in their environment like when you rearrange the furniture or bring new items into the house.

O o

P p

P is for Purr

How cats purr no one is sure.
Jungle cats can only roar.
Why cats purr is evident.
They're relaxed and happy and content.

All small cats and some bigger cats, like the ocelot and cheetah, make a steady, rhythmic sound called purring. Many of the big cats can only roar. There are several explanations for how cats purr. One attributes purring to the vibration of a set of additional or false vocal chords as a cat inhales and exhales. Another theorizes that the sound results from increased blood flow resonating through the chest, throat, and head.

A mother cat greets her kittens with purring. Cat owners all experience the comfort of a purring cat on the lap. Cats purr in response to petting and stroking. Cats purr while napping.

Although we usually associate purring with contentment, cats also purr when they are injured, having kittens, or dying. Some speculate that purring may have a healing function, making it appropriate to express pleasure as well as to soothe pain.

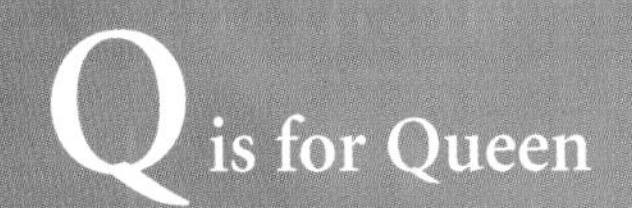 is for Queen

Things to remember to teach your young:
Catch with the claws and wash with the tongue.
Pounce on the mouse and hunt the rat.
Make each kitten a clever cat.

A female cat, particularly a mother cat, is called a *queen* (a male cat is a *tom*). Mother cats have a strong maternal bond with their kittens. As solitary animals a mother cat receives little help in the wild in raising her young. She must be the source for all food, safety, and lessons on how to survive in the wild.

A mother cat will move her kittens if she feels they are in danger. A mother cat in Brooklyn, New York, became famous when she rescued her five kittens from a blazing fire, getting her paws and coat burned and her eyes blistered shut. Named Scarlett by her rescuers, she dashed back into the flames for each kitten and carried them out one by one. At the end she touched each with her nose to count and make sure she had them all.

Kittens learn to hunt, climb, and clean themselves from their mothers. Domestic mother cats also teach their kittens proper social behavior, including use of the litter box and how to interact with humans and other cats.

R r

R is for Rescue

He came in muddy and covered with mites.
He was skinny and hungry and scarred from fights.
Now he's plump and sassy and smug and sleek.
He owns the house. It took a week.

Hundreds of local and regional humane groups devote their energies to rescuing homeless and neglected cats. They provide food and medical attention, seek adoptive homes for abandoned cats, and educate people about cat welfare.

Some rescue organizations work exclusively to trap, spay or neuter, vaccinate, and return (TNR) feral cats. Feral cats are domestic cats that were either born or became wild. Large colonies of feral cats pose problems in urban areas. Once these cats were caught and destroyed, but more communities are adopting the TNR policy, funding the medical care through civic organizations and volunteers.

People often import or purchase big and exotic cats without understanding how unsuitable they are as household pets. Big and exotic cat sanctuaries provide lifelong homes for these animals which give them the space, care, and setting they need to live healthy lives.

Abused or neglected cats require patience and care to blend into a new household. Giving a loving home to a rescued cat can be especially rewarding. Love and care can make a shy and timid creature a lifelong friend.

Sharp, curved claws give cats the perfect tool for climbing, digging, fighting, and capturing prey. Cats keep their claws in good condition by scratching objects around them. Scratching doesn't sharpen a cat's pointed claws; it keeps them in good shape by removing the dead outer layer. Scratching also helps a cat establish its turf by activating the paws' scent glands to mark its domain by smell as well as visible claw marks.

Scratching is instinctive, natural behavior. When your cat starts to shred your new couch, don't try to punish it. Cats do not understand or respond to punishment. Provide a scratching post and encourage your cat to use it to redirect scratching activities to more appropriate objects.

No one can doubt that a cat derives pure pleasure from both scratching and stretching. Cats stretch to maintain flexibility and keep in tone. No wonder a famous yoga pose is called the "cat stretch."

S s

S is for Scratching and Stretching

It's rare a cat will run and fetch.
(That's for dogs.) They'd rather stretch
and yawn and saunter out
to stop and sniff and scratch about.

T is for Tail and Toes

Silently on dainty feet,
taking steps precise and neat.
With a leap defying gravity's laws,
she lands upon her padded paws.

Tt

Cats' long, supple tails aid in balance for walking, running, and leaping. Some breeds, the Manx, Japanese Bobtail, and Cymric, have no tails or short, stump-like tails. Tails also communicate mood. An upright tail signals a friendly greeting; a low, swishing tail indicates an angry cat.

Cats are digitigrades, meaning they walk on their toes. This increases speed and length of stride, aiding their ability to hunt. Cats are also amazingly athletic with powerful back legs giving them the ability to jump with strength and accuracy. An organ in its inner ear (the vestibular apparatus) gives a cat its acute sense of balance.

Cats *do not* always land on their feet but they do have a "righting reflex" which helps them to orient themselves in unexpected falls to land safely. Cats have an unusually flexible spine and no collarbone. This, along with its tail and the ear's vestibular apparatus, allows a cat to rotate in midair and right itself, landing on padded paws and avoiding injury. Even when cats right themselves, falls can result in serious injuries so be careful to secure windows, doors, and balconies.

U is for Understand

Our cats can tell us how they feel.
Their eyes, their ears, their tails reveal
their moods, their thoughts, what they have planned.
If we watch, we'll understand.

Understanding is the center of any good relationship. Cats use body language to communicate their moods with us as well as with other cats.

Cat body language involves posture, tail position, face, whiskers, ears, eyes, and fur. A friendly cat comes toward you with tail up, ears and head forward, confident and relaxed. Cats will also rub or bump their heads against you or one another in a friendly greeting. This allows them to mark their scent and gives them an opportunity to sniff out your identity. A cat flopping over and showing you his tummy is telling you he feels safe and happy.

Nervous or fearful cats appear tentative with their tails low and wrapped under them. Cats arch their backs and puff up their fur to look bigger and more intimidating in order to defend themselves when threatened.

A twitching tail means trouble is brewing, and when its ears are flattened and its tail thrashes back and forth, the cat is really angry.

Learn to read the signals to better understand what your cat is trying to say.

Uu

Good cat care involves an annual visit to your veterinarian for vaccinations and a general checkup. Veterinarians are medical professionals educated in animal health to treat sick and injured animals, and work with people to raise happy and healthy pets.

Your cat can't tell you when it's not feeling well. Lack of interest in food, changes in appearance or habits (including litter box habits), lameness, persistent coughing, sneezing, vomiting or diarrhea merit a call to the vet. Be sure to use a pet carrier for trips to the vet.

What should you expect when you take your cat to the vet? Your vet will take and record your pet's medical history and may ask you about your cat's diet, personality, environment, and habits. A good physical exam will include checking the skin and coat, eyes, ears, and mouth, and feeling the abdomen to check internal organs. Your vet will listen to your cat's heart and lungs through a stethoscope and take its temperature. Your vet is an expert in handling the most nervous and shy cat.

V v

V is for Veterinarian

Make your cat's life full and long.
Keep her healthy, fit, and strong.
Take her for a checkup where
your vet will give her expert care.

Cats and kittens require vaccinations against infectious diseases. Your vet will recommend the proper vaccinations and time schedule depending on the region you live in and your pet's lifestyle. A visit to the vet is a good time to ask questions about cat care and health. Your vet can give tips on diet and show how to do things like clip claws or give any needed medications. If further tests and treatment are required, your vet will explain the health concern and recommend a course of action.

Because of pet overpopulation, veterinarians and humane organizations recommend spaying and neutering to prevent unwanted litters. These safe, simple surgeries leave a cat unable to reproduce. Spayed and neutered cats tend to have longer, healthier lives and calmer personalities.

Becoming a veterinarian requires a major commitment to study and hard work. You need to be a good student in general science, math, and biology, as well as being an animal lover. If you like working with people and animals, a career as a veterinary technician or assistant may also be a good choice for you.

W is for Whiskers

Whiskers, there are twenty-four,
guide a cat around the door.
In the dark and on the stair,
sensing currents in the air.

A cat's fur coat protects it from the elements regulating body temperature. The technical name for whiskers is *vibrissae*. There are three other types of hair that make up a cat's fur coat. **Down** hairs (closest to the skin) provide warmth. **Awn** hairs in the middle coat insulate. The **guard** hairs provide a topcoat, keeping a cat dry and snug.

Whiskers are long, stiff hairs, twice as thick as the other hairs. They are embedded deep in the cat's skin where there are special nerve endings. Cats have 24 whiskers on their upper lip; 12 on each side arranged in four horizontal rows. Cats also have whiskers on their chins and above their eyes.

Whiskers help cats navigate in the dark, essential for hunting at night, and help them sense changes in air currents as they approach objects. That's how a cat knows where an obstacle may be without seeing it and can carefully step around it. Blind cats (unable to survive in the wild) can live comfortable lives indoors using their whiskers, as well as their keen sense of smell, to guide their way around the house.

W

W

X

X marks the spot

Sometimes you hardly know she's there,
washing after meals with care.
Scratching in the box of litter,
a cat's a clean and quiet critter.

Edward Lowe invented the first commercially available cat litter in Michigan in 1947. Cat litters are made from clay or silica gel, as well as biodegradable pellets containing recycled paper, wood shavings, bran, or corncobs.

Cats are naturally clean, quiet, and adjust easily to indoor life. Their instinctive use of a litter tray makes cats perfect pets for people who live in high-rise apartments and households where all the adults work. If your cat starts avoiding the litter box, take it to the vet to make sure there isn't a medical problem. Litter problems can be prevented by keeping the cat box clean and accessible, away from human traffic and a cat's food dish. Multi-cat owners need to ensure they have enough litter boxes, following the simple rule of one more box than there are cats in a household.

Less susceptible to disease, accident, and injury, indoor cats tend to live longer. And keeping cats indoors helps prevent the destruction of local and endangered birds and small animals. Cats who enjoy the outdoors should wear collars with identifying tags as well as a warning bell.

Y y

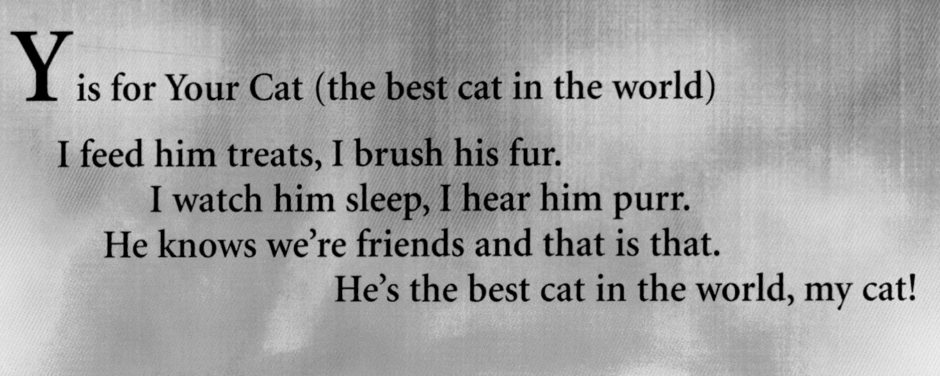

Y is for Your Cat (the best cat in the world)

I feed him treats, I brush his fur.
I watch him sleep, I hear him purr.
He knows we're friends and that is that.
He's the best cat in the world, my cat!

Which cat is the best cat in the world? Why, your cat, of course!

We love our cats, care for and protect them. Charles Lindbergh, the famous aviator, took his cat Patsy with him on many flights but not on his famous first trip across the Atlantic saying: "It's too dangerous a journey to risk the cat's life."

Adopting a cat is making a commitment to its well-being for its lifetime. Your cat is an intelligent, sensitive creature that will depend on you for its care for the 16 or more years of its life. You can do a lot to ensure your cat's contentment, safety, and health.

The simple joy of sharing your day creates an intimate bond between you and your cat. Petting and playing with your cat strengthens that bond and gives your pet exercise and mental stimulation. Cats love to chase balls, bat at feathers, wands, and teasers. They attack catnip mice and sometimes your shoelaces. Most cats like their heads and foreheads stroked and to be scratched under the chin. When a cat has had too much petting, it may give a gentle nip and run away.

If you take your cat with you on a family trip, make sure you use a carrier and have plenty of water and a litter container. Get a collar with an identification tag with your name and contact information in case your cat gets lost. And because of the danger of overheating, never leave your cat unattended in a parked car.

Some household cleaners and chemicals are poisonous to cats; so are chocolate and acetaminophen. Make sure these are safely stored away from your cat's reach. Danger may also come from the natural world as certain houseplants, for example, an Easter lily, are poisonous.

Adopting a young kitten is a lot of fun but takes more time and care to train. Children need to know that kittens are very fragile and must be handled with care.

When your cat curls next to you for a cozy nap or slowly blinks its eyes at you, it is showing its trust in you and its happiness with its friend for life.

Cats sleep 12-16 hours a day, more than most mammals and twice as much as humans. Cats sleep to save energy for hunting. To be efficient predators, cats need short spurts of energy to generate the speed and strength needed to capture prey. Domestic cats, fed at home, have no need to hunt; yet they are ruled by the genetic code of their ancestors.

Because their body temperature drops during sleep, cats like warm places for napping—sunny spots, a warm lap, or near a heater. To conserve heat cats curl themselves into tight balls, paws tucked in, and tails touching noses. As they get warmer their posture changes, stretching out to become cooler.

Most naps are light sleep where a cat is poised to wake quickly and respond to danger in the wild or the sound of a can opener at home. That's why we say a person is "cat napping" when taking a short snooze. About a quarter of resting is in deep sleep.

Do cats dream? That's something they cannot tell us; however, in periods of deep sleep their paws and faces often twitch.

Z
Z

Z is for ZZZZs

Paws tucked in and breathing deep,
curled up tight and fast asleep.
Cats nap all day or so it seems.
There must be mice in kittens' dreams.

Cat Stats and Feline Facts

Cat Chat

- Catnip is an herb of the mint family that appeals to many cats, putting them into a playful and sometimes trancelike state. Big cats like catnip as much as our house cats do. Some zoos give their big cats catnip to stimulate their interest and enrich their environment.

- There are special words for groups of animals—a group of cats is a clowder, a group of kittens is a litter (usually from one mother) or a kindle. An average litter produces three to six kittens.

- Cats sun themselves not just for warmth but to get the vitamin D sunshine provides.

- Never feed your cat dog food. Dog food does not contain the essential nutrients cats need.

- Not all cats hate water. Tigers love to swim. The Turkish Van breed of domestic cat, known as the "swimming cat," is originally from the Lake Van region of Turkey.

- Cats can reproduce very quickly. Female cats can have two to three litters each year. According to the National Human Education Society one female and mate and all their surviving offspring producing two litters a year can produce as many as 66,000 cats in six years.

Cats respond best to names that end in an "ee" sound. The American Society for the Prevention of Cruelty to Animals (ASPCA) surveyed veterinarians to find out which pet names are most popular.

1. Max
2. Sam
3. Lady
4. Bear
5. Smokey
6. Shadow
7. Kitty
8. Molly
9. Buddy
10. Brandy

The first Siamese cat in the United States came as a gift to President Rutherford B. Hayes in 1878 from the American Consul in Bangkok. Many U. S. presidents have had First Cats live with them in the White House. Here are some of them:

Abraham Lincoln	*Tabby*
Rutherford B. Hayes	*Siam*
Theodore Roosevelt	*Slippers, Tom Quartz*
Calvin Coolidge	*Tiger, Smokey, Blackie*
John Kennedy	*Tom Kitten*
Gerald Ford	*Shan*
Jimmy Carter	*Mist Malarky Ying Yang*
Ronald Reagan	*Cleo, Sara*
Bill Clinton	*Socks*
George W. Bush	*India (called Willie)*

Physical Facts

Fastest land animal: the Cheetah (*Acinonyx jubatus*) can reach speeds of 62 mph or 100 kph.

Life expectancy for domestic cat: 15 to 20 years (Life expectancy for cats has nearly doubled since 1930 when it was 8 years.)

How old is my cat in human years?

Cat Years	Human Years
4 months	7 years
6 months	10 years
8 months	13 years
1 year	15 years
2	24
4	32
6	40
8	48
10	56
12	64
14	72
16	80
18	88
20	96
22	100

Largest domestic breed: Maine Coon

Smallest domestic breed: Singapura

Most popular breeds: Persian, Siamese, Maine Coon

- Cats have 290 bones and 517 muscles in their bodies. Of these, 30 muscles are in each ear, which they use to pivot their ears 180 degrees.
- Cats have 30 teeth: 16 on the top jaw and 14 on the bottom.
- Cats have five toes on the front paws, four on the back. Polydactyl cats are born with extra toes.
- Cat nose pads are like human fingerprints; each is unique.
- Cats' hearts beat twice as fast as humans.
- A cat's tongue feels like sandpaper because it is lined with backward hooks called papillae to help in grooming and eating flesh off bones.
- What do cats have in common with giraffes and camels? They are the only animals that walk moving both left feet together, then both right feet together. This makes them swift and silent.
- Cats don't like the smells of vinegar, orange, or lemon rinds.

Helen L. Wilbur

Former librarian Helen L. Wilbur has loved cats all her life. Most of her cats have been rescued from the streets of New York. In explaining her goal in writing an animal book for children, she says "Animals don't care if you aren't the most popular kid in the class or whether you did your homework." She has a BA in English Language and Literature from the University of Chicago and a master's degree in library science from Columbia University. Helen lives in New York City.

Robert Papp

Drawing and painting since a boy, Robert Papp was formally trained at DuCret School of Art in New Jersey. His award-winning artwork includes hundreds of illustrations for major publishers across the United States, but Robert says he is most proud of the reaction he gets from the children who view his work and always seem to notice each and every brushstroke. His first children's book, *The Scarlet Stockings Spy*, was named an IRA Teachers' Choice in 2005. *M is for Meow* is his third book with Sleeping Bear Press. Robert lives in historic Bucks County, Pennsylvania, with his artist wife, Lisa, and their orange cat, Taffy.